Dec. 2001

Mary~

To a wonderful friend who shares the same appreciation for great words of comfort. Enjoy, during your personal time and/or share them with family and friends!

Love,
Carla Jo

P9-DFZ-097

LITTLE MIRACLES

Compiled by
Dan Zadra with Katie Lambert

☆

Designed by
Kobi Yamada and Steve Potter

COM·PEN'DI·UM™
INCORPORATED

PUBLISHING & COMMUNICATIONS
SEATTLE, WASHINGTON

ACKNOWLEDGEMENTS

These quotations were gathered lovingly but unscientifically over several years and/or contributed by many friends and clients. Some arrived–and survived in our files–on scraps of paper and may therefore be imperfectly worded or attributed. To the authors, contributors and original sources, our thanks, and where appropriate, our apologies. –The Editors

WITH SPECIAL THANKS TO

Gerry Baird, Beth Bingham, Josie and Rob Estes, Dawn Ewing, Jennifer Hurwitz, Dick Kamm, Beth Keane, Liam Lavery, Teri O'Brien, Janet Potter & Family, Diane Roger, John Schilling, Robert & Val Yamada, Tote Yamada, Annie Zadra, Augie & Rosie Zadra and August and Arline Zadra.

CREDITS

Compiled by Dan Zadra with Katie Lambert.
Designed by Kobi Yamada and Steve Potter.

Printed in Hong Kong

CHERISHED
MESSAGES OF HOPE,
JOY, LOVE, KINDNESS
AND COURAGE.

EXPECT A MIRACLE

Dr. Jo Blessing tells of an elderly patient who experienced a minor miracle in her life.

Despondent over the death of her only son, the old woman tidied up her little apartment one morning. On her nightstand she sprinkled out the sleeping pills. Then she trudged to her favorite place, a public park on the corner, where she sat alone, summoning the resolve she would need to end her life.

At noon something happened that changed her mind. Along came a man in an expensive-looking business suit. He was about the same age as her son, and he appeared to be in a hurry. For no particular reason, however, he suddenly stopped, smiled and stayed a few minutes to feed the pigeons with her. When he left, he touched her arm and said, "Good-bye—I can't remember when I've had a nicer time. Take good care of our little birds." He did not know that his kindness had restored her will to live.

Today, without even realizing it, you may be the answer to someone's prayers. Don't worry about whether you believe in miracles; just believe that your touch, your thoughtfulness, and your love really do work wonders in the lives of others.

Someone you know—a friend, neighbor, loved one, co-worker or family member—may be hurting, doubting, wondering or struggling. Give them this book; tell them that you're pulling for them, and that you believe in them. Tonight, call someone you care about. Tell them you miss them; tell them you're sorry. Arrange a visit. Make some lemonade or coffee. Take a walk. Enjoy the sun. Eat a popsicle. Feed the birds. Laugh, hug, cry. Invite a little miracle into your life. They are everywhere, and all around you.

Dan Zadra

INVITE ☆ EXPECT ☆ RECEIVE ☆ ENJOY

GIVE THANKS
FOR UNKNOWN
BLESSINGS ALREADY
ON THEIR WAY.

—Native American saying

INVITE ☆ EXPECT ☆ RECEIVE ☆ ENJOY

$\mathcal{T}$he story's about you.

–HORACE

$\mathcal{D}$o not wait for life.
Do not long for it. Be aware, always
and at every moment, that the miracle
is in the here and now.

–MARCEL PROUST

$\mathcal{Y}$ou are alive, and that is the only
place we need to be to start.

–CARRIE RAINEY

LITTLE MIRACLES™

*T*ime is a very precious gift—
so precious that it is only given to
us moment by moment.

–AMELIA BARR

☆

*E*ach instant is a place
we've never been.

–MARK STRAND

☆

*T*here is always one
unexpected moment in life when a
door opens to let the future in.

–GRAHAM GREENE

*T*hink…of the world
you carry within you.

–Rainer Maria Rilke

*Y*ou are not called to be a
canary in a cage. You are called
to be an eagle, and to fly sun
to sun, over continents.

–Henry Ward Beecher

*Y*our aspirations
are your possibilities.

–Samuel Johnson

LITTLE MIRACLES™

9

$\mathcal{L}$ife is a promise, fulfill it.
–MOTHER TERESA

☆

$\mathcal{Y}$ou are the one and only you that
ever was, or ever will be. What you
are going to do with this miracle is
a question only you can answer.
–DAN ZADRA

☆

$\mathcal{E}$mbrace your uniqueness.
Time is much too short to be
living someone else's life.
–KOBI YAMADA

*T*here is nothing that
has to be done—there is
only someone to be.

–JACQUELYN SMALL

*E*veryone has a unique role to fill
in the world and is important in some
respect. Everyone, including and perhaps
especially you, is indispensable.

–NATHANIEL HAWTHORNE

*D*o not wish to be anything but what
you are, and to be that perfectly.

–ST. FRANCIS DE SALES

$\mathcal{T}$he great use of life is
to spend it for something
that will outlast it.

–WILLIAM JAMES

$\mathcal{W}$e are called upon to become
creators, to make the world new and
in that sense to bring something into
being which was not there before.

–JOHN ELOF BOODIN

$\mathcal{C}$reativity is God's gift to you.
What you do with it is your gift to God.

–BOB MOAWAD

*W*e become happier,
much happier, when we realize
that life is an opportunity rather
than an obligation.

–MARY AUGUSTINE

*T*oday is your day and mine,
the only day we have, the day in which
we play our part—and the whole world is
starting to feel it all at once. It is no time
for cynicism. This is our time to
grow and build and love.

–ELIE SHULMAN

EVERY BLADE OF GRASS

HAS AN ANGEL THAT BENDS

OVER IT AND WHISPERS,

"GROW! GROW!"

–The Talmud

INVITE ☆ EXPECT ☆ RECEIVE ☆ ENJOY

$\mathcal{T}$here came a time when the risk to remain tight in a bud was more painful than the risk it took to blossom.

–ANAIS NIN

$\mathcal{W}$hy stay we on earth except to grow?

–ROBERT BROWNING

$\mathcal{W}$e must be willing to relinquish the life we've planned, so as to have the life that is waiting for us.

–JOSEPH CAMPBELL

*I*t is only by risking from
one hour to another that we live at all.
–WILLIAM JAMES

*N*ot to dream boldly may
turn out to be simply irresponsible.
–GEORGE LEONARD

*D*o not pray for dreams
equal to your powers. Pray for
powers equal to your dreams.
–ADELAIDE ANN PROCTER

$\mathcal{Y}$our dreams grow
holy put into action.
–ADELAIDE ANN PROCTER

$\mathcal{S}$omewhere someone is looking
for exactly what you have to offer.
–LOUISE L. HAY

$\mathcal{Y}$our work is to discover your work,
and then, with all your heart,
to give yourself to it.
–BUDDHA

LITTLE MIRACLES™

*E*nthusiasm is a kind of
faith that has been set on fire.
–GEORGE MATTHEW ADAMS

*T*he mind determines what's possible.
The soul surpasses it.
–PILAR COOLINTA

*W*e never know how good we are,
until we are called to rise.
–EMILY DICKINSON

$\mathcal{W}$e were not sent into
this world to do anything into
which we cannot put our hearts.
–JOHN RUSKIN

$\mathcal{T}$hat is the simple secret.
Always take your heart to work.
–MERYL STREEP

$\mathcal{B}$e faithful to that which exists
nowhere but in yourself.
–ANDRE GIDE

LITTLE MIRACLES™

*J*ust as there are no
little people or unimportant lives,
there is no insignificant work.

—ELENA BONNER

*I*f I hadn't taken up painting,
I would have raised chickens.
It's all art.

—GRANDMA MOSES

*I*t is possible, as you know, to make
a great painting on a small canvas.

—C.D. WARNER

LITTLE MIRACLES™

$\mathscr{I}$t is often merely
for an excuse that we say
things are impossible.

–F. DE LA ROCHEFOUCALD

$\mathscr{I}$t is not impossibilities which fill us
with the deepest despair, but possibilities
which we have failed to realize.

–ROBERT MALLET

$\mathscr{A}$las for those who never sing,
but die with all their music in them.

–OLIVER WENDELL HOLMES

LITTLE MIRACLES™

I've learned that minor miracles are fairly common in the work-a-day world. Try long enough and hard enough to do wonderful work and, sure enough, you occasionally work wonders.

–STEVEN SPIELBERG

*W*hen we do the best we can, we never know what miracle is wrought in our life, or in the life of another.

–HELEN KELLER

NOW YOU JUST
BELIEVE. THAT IS ALL
YOU HAVE TO DO—
JUST BELIEVE.

—Advice from an old Ohio farmer

INVITE ☆ EXPECT ☆ RECEIVE ☆ ENJOY

$\mathcal{T}$o me, faith means not worrying.

–JOHN DEWEY

$\mathcal{W}$orry is a
misuse of the imagination.

–DAN ZADRA

$\mathcal{F}$aith and love are
your natural inheritance. Fear is
an invention of the mind.

–GERALD JAMPOLSKY

*F*ear, too, is a type of faith—
faith that it won't work out.

–SISTER MARY TRICKY

*T*rust your hopes.

–FATHER BILLINGS, S.J.

*I*f you do not hope, you will not
find what is beyond your hopes.

–ST. CLEMENT

LITTLE MIRACLES™

25

*S*ome things have to
be believed to be seen.

–Mark Victor Hansen

*T*he world was made round
so we would never be able to see
too far down the road.

–Isak Dinesen

*P*atience! Does the windmill
stray in search of the wind?

–Andy Sklivis

$\mathcal{E}$ven if your efforts
seem for years to be producing
no result, one day a light that
is in exact proportion to them
will flood your soul.

–SIMONE WEIL

$\mathcal{L}$et nothing dim
the light that shines from within.

–MAYA ANGELOU

$\mathcal{T}$o build in darkness does require faith. But one day the light returns and you discover that you have become a fortress which is impregnable to certain kinds of trouble; you may even find yourself needed and sought by others as a beacon in their dark.

–OLGA ROSMANITH

$\mathcal{W}$hat is to give light must endure burning.

–VICTOR FRANKL

$\mathcal{N}$othing worth doing is
completed in our lifetime; therefore
we must be saved by hope. Nothing
we do can be fully appreciated alone;
therefore we must be saved by love.
Nothing true or beautiful or good makes
total sense in any context of history;
therefore we are saved by faith.

–REINHOLD NIEBUHR

$\mathcal{F}$ear knocked at the door.
Faith answered. No one was there.

–INSCRIPTION AT HIND'S HEAD INN, ENGLAND

THERE DOES,
IN FACT, APPEAR
TO BE A PLAN.

–Albert Einstein

INVITE ☆ EXPECT ☆ RECEIVE ☆ ENJOY

We talk about finding
God…as if He could get lost.

–JEROME HORTON

People see God every day,
they just don't recognize him.

–PEARL BAILEY

A coincidence may be God's way
of acting anonymously in your life.

–ANONYMOUS

$\mathcal{T}$he feeling remains that
He is on the journey too.

–TERESA OF AVILLA

" $\mathcal{F}$or I know the plans
I have for you; plans to prosper
you and not to harm you, plans to
give you hope and a future."

–JEREMIAH 29:11

$\mathcal{A}$ll I have seen
teaches me to trust the Creator
for all I have not seen.

–RALPH WALDO EMERSON

*W*hat you call holy,
we call love.

−LETTER TO A MISSIONARY FROM THE SENECA INDIANS

*E*ach of us is loved,
as if there were only one of us.

−ST. AUGUSTINE

*G*od loves you…
whether you like it or not.

−BUMPERSTICKER

LITTLE MIRACLES™

I can't explain it.
All I know is that prayer works.
—Norman Cousins

*T*o those who believe,
no explanation is necessary;
to those who do not believe,
no explanation is possible.
—The Song of Bernadette

*T*hey often pray best, who do not
know they are praying.
—Unknown

$\mathscr{G}$od, give me guts.

–Eli Mygatt

$\mathscr{W}$e were not created
to be eaten by anxiety, but to
walk erect, free, unafraid in a world
where there is work to do, truth to
seek, love to give and win.

–Joseph Ford Newton

$\mathcal{A}$t night I turn
my problems over to God.
He's going to be up
all night anyway.

–CARRIE WESTINGSON

$\mathcal{B}$elieve there is a great
power silently working all things
for good, behave yourself and
never mind the rest.

–BEATRIX POTTER

To believe in immortality is one thing, but first believe in life.

–*Robert Louis Stevenson*

$\mathcal{Y}$ou have to take time to live.
Living takes time.

–ELEANOR MCMILLEN BROWN

$\mathcal{T}$ime is God's way of keeping everything from happening all at once.

–UNKNOWN

$\mathcal{H}$old every moment sacred.
Give each its true and due fulfillment.

–THOMAS MANN

LITTLE MIRACLES™

$\mathscr{E}$arth is crammed with heaven.

–ELIZABETH BARRETT BROWNING

$\mathscr{F}$irst comes life, then love,
then understanding.

–MARGE PIERCY

$\mathscr{W}$e come. We go.
And in between we try
to understand.

–ROD STEIGER

In each of us
there is a little of all of us.

–D. LICHTENBERG

*Wh*at lies behind us and what lies
before us are tiny matters compared
to what lies within us.

–RALPH WALDO EMERSON

I was never less
alone than while by myself.

–EDWARD GIBBON

$\mathcal{T}$he next message you need
is always right where you are.

–RAM DASS

$\mathcal{W}$henever you need one,
a teacher will appear.

–SENECA

$\mathcal{T}$eachers point to the door,
but you must enter by yourself.

–CHINESE PROVERB

*S*ome of life's greatest
lessons cannot be pried from books—
they must be experienced
in your bones.

–KOBI YAMADA

*S*omebody showed it to me
and I found it by myself.

–LEW WELCH

*N*othing is more exciting
and rewarding than the sudden
flash of insight that leaves
you a changed person.

–ARTHUR GORDON

LITTLE MIRACLES™

$\mathcal{T}$he delights of self-discovery
are always available.

–GAIL SHEEHY

$\mathcal{I}$ loaf and invite my soul.

–WALT WHITMAN

$\mathcal{W}$ho looks outside, dreams.
Who looks inside, awakes.

–CARL JUNG

$\mathscr{O}$ne small step
up the mountain often widens
your horizon in all directions.

−E.H. GRIGGS

$\mathscr{I}$t is by tiny steps
that we ascend the stars.

−JACK LEEDSTROM

$\mathscr{R}$aise your hopes and expectations
high enough, and you shall touch
wings with the divine.

−CELIA MORA

$\mathcal{W}$e're always trying to
move out of the darkness,
when all we have to do
is turn on the light.

–STEVE POTTER

$\mathcal{W}$hen you come to the edge of
all the light you have, and must take a
step into the darkness of the unknown,
believe that one of two things will
happen. Either there will be something
solid for you to stand on–or you
will be taught how to fly.

–PATRICK OVERTON

ALWAYS KNOW
IN YOUR HEART THAT
YOU ARE FAR BIGGER THAN
ANYTHING THAT CAN
HAPPEN TO YOU.

–Dan Zadra

INVITE ☆ EXPECT ☆ RECEIVE ☆ ENJOY

$\mathscr{E}$verything in this life has a purpose.
There are no mistakes, no coincidences.
All events are blessings given
to us to learn from.

–ELIZABETH KUBLER-ROSS

$\mathscr{P}$roblems, too, have their purpose.
They are necessary for health.
Be grateful for them.

–ST. FRANCIS DE SALES

"$\mathscr{W}$hat is the heaviest burden?"
asked the child. "To have nothing to
carry," answered the old man.

–UNKNOWN

I've never been one who thought
the Lord should make life easy; I've just
asked Him to make me strong.

–EVA BOWRING

*O*ne should take children's
philosophy to heart. They do not
despise a bubble because it bursts.
They immediately set to work
to blow another one.

–KEYNOTE

*A*h, if only you knew the peace
there is in an accepted sorrow.

–JEANNE DE LA MOTTE-GUYTON

$\mathscr{Y}$ou are more important
than your problems.

–JOSE FERRER

$\mathscr{O}$ut of every crises comes
the chance to be reborn.

–NENA O'NEILL

$\mathscr{T}$hings fall apart so that things
can fall together.

–DAN ZADRA

$\mathcal{W}$hen you're down
to nothing, remember that you
really do have the power to make
something out of nothing.

–DON WARD

$\mathcal{E}$ven when the friendly lights
go out, there will be a light by
which your heart sees.

–OLGA ROSMANITH

$\mathcal{A}$mazing how we can
light tomorrow with today.

–ELIZABETH BARRETT BROWNING

LITTLE MIRACLES™

GOOD FRIEND,
ALWAYS BE OPEN TO
THE MIRACLE OF THE
SECOND CHANCE.

—Rev. David Stier

*T*here will come a time when
you believe everything is finished.
That will be the beginning.

–LOUIS L'AMOUR

*N*ever despair.

–HORACE

*T*o deem any situation
impossible is to make it so.

–BERNARD DRUMMOND

LITTLE MIRACLES™

*K*now in your heart that
all things are possible.

–Dan Zadra

*T*here is always, always,
always a way.

–Dr. Robert Schuller

*N*ever give up on anything or anybody.
Miracles happen every day.

–H. Jackson Brown

*W*e couldn't conceive of a
miracle if none had ever happened.
—LIBBIE FUDIM

*T*he idea that nothing is true except
what we comprehend is ridiculous.
—WINSTON CHURCHILL

*I*f I were absolutely certain
about all things, I would be fearful
of losing my way. But since everything
and anything are always possible, the
miraculous is always nearby and
wonders shall never, ever cease.
—ROBERT FULGHUM

LITTLE MIRACLES™

$\mathcal{W}$hat we need is
more people who specialize
in the impossible.
–THEODORE ROETHKE

$\mathcal{T}$he unexpected and the
incredible belong in this world.
Only then is life whole.
–CARL GUSTAV JUNG

$\mathcal{W}$hen nothing is sure,
everything is possible.
—LIBBIE FUDIM

"*But* I can't believe impossible things,"
cried Alice. "Of course you can, child,"
responded the Queen. "Why, sometimes
I've believed six impossible things
before breakfast!"

–LEWIS CARROL

There are only two ways to live your life.
One is as though nothing is a miracle.
The other is as though everything is a miracle.

–ALBERT EINSTEIN

The moment you move out of the way,
you make room for the miracle to take place.

–DR. BARBARA KING

$\mathcal{W}$here there is great love
there are always miracles.

–WILLA CATHER

$\mathcal{J}$ust as angels are attracted to the light
of joy and kindness, so too are miracles
attracted to the lamp of faith and love.

–MARY AUGUSTINE

$\mathcal{S}$omeday all you'll have to light
the way will be a single ray of hope—
and that will be enough.

–KOBI YAMADA

A FRIEND
WALKS IN WHEN
THE WHOLE WORLD
WALKS OUT.

—Unknown

INVITE ☆ EXPECT ☆ RECEIVE ☆ ENJOY

*P*eople come into
your life for a reason, a season or
a lifetime. When you figure out which
it is, you know exactly what to do.

–MICHELLE VENTOR

*W*e all go about
longing for kindred spirits.
To meet a stranger and, in the first
few seconds, to be able to guess
everything of any importance
about each other—well, this is
not a stranger at all.

–PILAR COOLINTA

LITTLE MIRACLES™

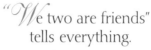

"We two are friends"
tells everything.

–E.V. LUCAS

Oh, the comfort, the inexpressible
comfort of feeling safe with a person;
having neither to weigh thoughts nor to
measure words but to pour them all out,
just as it is, chaff and grain together,
knowing that a faithful hand will take
and sift them, keeping what is worth
keeping, and then, with the breath of
kindness, blow the rest away.

–GEORGE ELIOT

$\mathcal{T}$he most beautiful discovery
true friends make is that they can
grow separately without growing apart.
–ELISABETH FOLEY

$\mathcal{T}$hough love be deeper,
friendship is more wide.
–CORINNE ROBINSON

$\mathcal{T}$he truth is, friendship is every
bit as sacred and eternal as marriage.
–KATHERINE MANSFIELD

LITTLE MIRACLES™

$\mathscr{F}$irst it is necessary to stand
on your own two feet. But the minute
you find yourself in that position, the
next thing you should do is reach out
your arms for a friend.

–KRISTIN HUNTER

$\mathscr{F}$riends are those rare souls
who ask how we are, and then
wait to hear the answer.

–ED CUNNINGHAM

$\mathscr{M}$y lifetime listens to yours.

–MURIEL RUCKEYSER

*D*ear George:
Remember, no man is a failure who
has friends. Thanks for the wings!
Love, Clarence the Angel

–IT'S A WONDERFUL LIFE

☆

*W*hatever our souls are made of,
yours and mine are the same.

–EMILY BRONTE

☆

*W*inter, spring, summer or fall…
all you've got to do is call…and I'll
be there, yes I will…you've got a friend.

–CAROLE KING

LITTLE MIRACLES™

CAME BUT FOR
FRIENDSHIP AND
TOOK AWAY LOVE.
—*Thomas Moore*

INVITE ☆ EXPECT ☆ RECEIVE ☆ ENJOY

$\mathcal{I}$ give thee what could not be
heard, what has not been given before:
The beat of my heart I give.

–EDITH M. THOMAS

$\mathcal{T}$wo people in love.
Two people taking their
souls out for a dance.

–KOBI YAMADA

$\mathcal{T}$hen we sat on the edge
of the earth, with our feet dangling
over the side, and marvelled that
we had found each other.

–ERIK DILLARD

There is no place love is not.
–HUGH PRATHER

Even when you are
a thousand miles away, I dine alone
with two cups on my table.
–JAPANESE LOVE LETTER

The story of love is not important.
What is important is that one is capable
of love. It is perhaps the only glimpse
we are permitted of eternity.
–HELEN HAYES

*N*ice how love creates an
'us' without destroying a 'me.'
–LEO BUSCAGLIA

*L*ove is a
game that two can play
and both can win.
–MICHAEL NOLAN

*N*o, the game
of love is never called on
account of darkness.
–TOTE YAMADA

*L*ove is what you've
been through with somebody.
–JAMES THURBER

*W*hen people love each
other, an important kind of
giving is "giving in."
–LEO BUSCAGLIA

*W*hat a world this would be if
we just built bridges instead of walls.
–CARLOS RAMIREZ

$\mathcal{L}$ove comes unseen;
we only see it go.

–Austin Dobson

$\mathcal{Y}$ou know a heart
can be broken, but it keeps on
beating just the same.

–Fannie Flagg

$\mathcal{L}$oving can cost a lot; not loving
always costs more.

–Merle Shain

$\mathcal{T}$here are only
four questions worth asking:
What is sacred? Of what is the
spirit made? What is worth living for?
What is worth dying for? The answer
to all four questions is the same:
Only love.

–DON JUAN DE MARCOS

$\mathcal{T}$here is no
surprise more magical than
the surprise of being loved.

–CHARLES MORGAN

$\mathcal{L}$ove cures people—
both the ones who give it and
the ones who receive it.

–DR. KARL MENNINGER

$\mathcal{T}$he conclusion is
always the same: love is the
most powerful and still the most
unknown energy of the world.

–PIERRE TEILHARD DE CHARDIN

$\mathscr{I}$t is safe to let the love in.
Love is your divine right.

–Louise L. Hay

$\mathscr{L}$ove without fear and
receive a glimpse of heaven.

–Unknown

$\mathscr{N}$ever mind the past.
Let our scars fall in love.

–Galway Kinnell

$\mathcal{L}$ove seeks
not limits but outlets.
–ANONYMOUS

$\mathcal{I}$f we want a love message
to be heard, it has to be sent out.
To keep a lamp burning, we have to
keep putting oil in it.
–MOTHER TERESA

$\mathcal{W}$here you find no love,
put love, and you will find love.
–JOHN OF THE CROSS

A BABY IS GOD'S
OPINION THAT THE
WORLD SHOULD
GO ON.

–Carl Sandburg

INVITE ☆ EXPECT ☆ RECEIVE ☆ ENJOY

"Where did I come from?"
the baby asked its mother.
She answered, half-crying, half-laughing,
and clasping the baby to her breast:
"You were hidden in my heart as
its desire, my darling. You were in the
dolls of all my childhood games.
In all my hopes and my loves, in my life,
in the life of my mother, and in her
mother before her, you have lived.
In the lap of the Eternal Spirit you
have been nursed and
anticipated for ages."

–RABINDRANATH TAGORE

$\mathcal{I}$t is no small thing when
children, who have so recently
come fresh from God, show
their love for us.

–KATHERINE MARSHALL

$\mathcal{C}$hildren are not poets.
They are too busy being poems.

–UNKNOWN

$\mathcal{C}$hildren are to be treated gently.
They are like snowflakes—unique,
but only here for awhile.

–KEYNOTE

$\mathscr{A}$ four-year-old boy gazed into the crib at his newborn baby sister and whispered to her, "Tell me again what God looks like—I'm starting to forget."

–ELIE WIEZCOFF

$\mathscr{I}$t is said, and it is true, that just before we are born, an angel puts a finger to our lips and says, "Hush, don't tell what you know." This is why we are born with a cleft on our upper lips and remembering nothing of where we came from.

–RODERICK MACLEISH

$\mathcal{W}$e only had one simple
rule in our home: Live harmlessly.

–SALLY BROWNE

$\mathcal{W}$hat a father or mother says to
their children is not heard by the world,
but it will be heard by posterity.

–JEAN PAUL RICHTER

$\mathcal{H}$elp a child
and you help humanity.

–PHILLIPS BROOKS

*I*n a child's lunchbox,
a mother's thought.

–JAPANESE PROVERB

*C*hildren will not remember you
for the material things you provided, but
for the feeling that you cherished them.

–GAIL GRENIER SWEET

*W*e didn't have much,
but we sure had plenty.

–SHERRY THOMAS

*L*ove, for Mama, was not something she thought or talked about.
It was something she lived in action.
She showed us, as Mother Teresa has,
that great love is found in sweeping a floor,
clearing a sink, caring for someone ill,
or offering a comforting embrace.

–LEO BUSCAGLIA

*D*ad showed his love
by taking a wing for himself and
leaving the drumsticks for us.

–DON WARD

LITTLE MIRACLES™

*E*ven now,
twenty-one years after my
father died, not a week goes by
that I don't find myself thinking
I should call him.

–HERB GARDNER

*T*reasure each other in
the recognition that we do not know
how long we will have each other.

–JOSHUA LIEBMAN

THE BEST AND MOST
BEAUTIFUL THINGS IN THE
WORLD CANNOT BE SEEN OR
EVEN TOUCHED. THEY MUST
BE FELT WITH THE HEART.

–Helen Keller

INVITE ☆ EXPECT ☆ RECEIVE ☆ ENJOY

$\mathcal{T}$he great lesson is that
the sacred is in the ordinary,
that it is to be found in one's
daily life, in one's neighbors, friends,
and family, in one's backyard.

–ABRAHAM MASLOW

$\mathcal{I}$t's good to have money and
the things that money can buy,
but it's good, too, to check up once in
a while and make sure you haven't lost
the things that money can't buy.

–GEORGE HORACE LORIMER

*J*ust think how happy
you'd be if you lost everything and
everyone you have right now—and then,
somehow got it back again.

–KOBI YAMADA

☆

*N*ormal day, let me
be aware of the treasure you are.
Let me learn from you, love you,
bless you before you depart.
Let me not pass you by in quest of
some rare and perfect tomorrow.

–UNKNOWN

𝓔ach of my days are miracles. I won't
waste my day; I won't throw away a miracle.
–Kelley Vickstrom

𝓦hen will you know you have enough,
and what will you do then?
–Barbara De Angelis, Ph.D

𝓘 have never been a millionaire.
But I have enjoyed a crackling fire, a
glorious sunset, a walk with a friend and
a hug from a child. There are plenty of
life's tiny delights for all of us.
–Jack Anthony

$\mathcal{T}$he most moving
moments of our lives find us
all without words.

–MARCEL MARCEAU

$\mathcal{I}$ live on earth where people
bless me for sneezing, but not for
living, laughing or singing.

–TOM HOPKINSON

$\mathcal{T}$he main thing is that we hear
and enjoy life's music everywhere.

–THEODORE FONTANE

LITTLE MIRACLES™

$\mathcal{N}$ot everything that counts
can be counted. Not everything
that can be counted counts.

–ALBERT EINSTEIN

$\mathcal{Y}$ou are more—much more—
than what you have.

–DON WILSON

$\mathcal{T}$ry measuring your
wealth by what you are rather than
what you have. Put the tape around
your heart rather than your head.

–KEYNOTE

$\mathcal{E}$nough is a feast.
–Celia Mora

$\mathcal{H}$e has achieved success who has
gained the love of little children; who
has left the world better than he found it;
who has never lacked appreciation of
earth's beauty; who has looked for the
best in others and given the best he had.
–A.J. Stanley

$\mathcal{W}$here there is too much,
something is missing.
–Hasidic Saying

*W*hen the most
important things in our life
happen we quite often do not know,
at the moment, what is going on.
—C.S. Lewis

*W*hen you have nothing left
but love, then for the first time you
become aware that love is enough.
—Unknown

*Y*ou are loved.
If so, what else matters?
—Edna St. Vincent Millay

LITTLE MIRACLES™

IF YOU REALLY
WANT TO BE HAPPY,
NOBODY CAN
STOP YOU.

–Sister Mary Tricky

INVITE ☆ EXPECT ☆ RECEIVE ☆ ENJOY

*J*oy is not in things;
it is in us.

–WAGNER

I asked for all things,
that I might enjoy life. I was given life,
that I might enjoy all things.

–KEYNOTE

*W*e are all happy if
we only knew it.

–FEODOR DOSTOEVSKY

$\mathcal{L}$earn to hold
loosely all that is not eternal.

–A. MAUDE ROYDEN

$\mathcal{E}$verything in life is most
fundamentally a gift. And you receive it
best, and you live it best, by holding it
with very open hands.

–LEO O'DONOVAN

$\mathcal{H}$ow many cares one loses when
one decides not to be something,
but to be someone.

–COCO CHANEL

LITTLE MIRACLES™

$\mathcal{C}$hoose to be happy.
It is a way of being wise.
–COLETTE

$\mathcal{I}$f you laugh a lot, when you
get older your wrinkles will be
in the right places.
–ANDREW MASON

$\mathcal{W}$e don't stop laughing
because we grow old–we grow old
because we stop laughing.
–MICHAEL PRITCHARD

A laugh is
a smile that bursts.

–MARY WALDRIP

*F*rom there to here,
and here to there, funny things
are everywhere.

–DR. SEUSS

*D*ogs laugh, but they laugh
with their tails.

–MAX EASTMAN

*W*here is the yesterday
that worried you so?

–CELIA MORA

I am an old man and
have known a great many
troubles, most of which have
never happened.

–MARK TWAIN

I am not afraid of tomorrow,
for I have seen yesterday and
I love today.

–WILLIAM ALLEN WHITE

*B*irds sing after a storm;
why shouldn't we?

–ROSE KENNEDY

*I*f children with terminal
cancer can find peace, joy and
laughter in their day—and they do—
why don't we?

–DAN ZADRA

*R*esolved, that I will take
each precious minute, and relish
all the joy within it.

–KATHLEEN RICE

LITTLE MIRACLES™

96

HOW WONDERFUL IT IS
THAT NOBODY NEED WAIT
A SINGLE MOMENT BEFORE
STARTING TO IMPROVE
THE WORLD.

–Anne Frank

INVITE ☆ EXPECT ☆ RECEIVE ☆ ENJOY

*B*ut where was I to start?
The world is so vast. I shall start
with the country I know best, my own.
But my country is so very large. I had
better start with my town. But my town,
too, is large. I had better start with my
street. No, my home. No, my family.
Never mind. I shall start with myself.

–ELIE WIESEL

*D*o not wait for leaders; do it alone,
person to person.

–MOTHER TERESA

LITTLE MIRACLES™

*T*he secret to happiness is to
plant trees under whose shade
you will never sit.

–NELSON HENDERSON

*R*eal generosity is doing
something nice for someone
who will never find out.

–FRANK A. CLARK

*O*ne must care about
a world one will never see.

–BERTRAND RUSSELL

$\mathscr{O}$ur world is saved,
one or two people at a time.

—ANDRE GIDE

$\mathscr{D}$o a deed of simple kindness,
Though its end you may not see,
It may reach, like widening ripples,
Down a long eternity.

—JAMES W. FOWLEY

$\mathscr{I}$f something comes to life in others
because of you, then you have made
an approach to immortality.

—NORMAN COUSINS

LITTLE MIRACLES™

$\mathcal{T}$he effect of one good-hearted
person is incalculable.

–OSCAR ARIAS

$\mathcal{W}$e must be the change
we wish to see in the world.

–MOHANDAS K. GANDHI

$\mathcal{W}$hen asked, "What can I do?"
I've found the answer frequently can
be found by rearranging the words
into the answer, "Do what I can."

–TEN MENTEN

$\mathcal{A}$ very important part
of the joy of living is
the joy of giving.

–WILLIAM BUCK

$\mathcal{C}$aring is everything.

–F. VONHUGEL

$\mathcal{Y}$ou have to reach
out your hand, that's what
it's there for.

–MACKINLEE BARTON

*G*ive what you have.
To someone, it may be better
than you dare to think.

–LONGFELLOW

*W*hat you are
accomplishing may seem like
a drop in the ocean. But if this
drop were not in the ocean,
it would be missed.

–MOTHER TERESA

FEELINGS
ARE EVERYWHERE.
BE GENTLE.

–J. Masai

INVITE ☆ EXPECT ☆ RECEIVE ☆ ENJOY

*W*hat a wonderful miracle,
if only we could look through
each other's eyes for an instant.

–THOREAU

*T*here is in each of us so much
goodness that if we could see its glow,
it would light the world.

–SAM FRIEND

*I*f we could hear one another's
prayers it would relieve God
of a great burden.

–MICHAEL NOLAN

LITTLE MIRACLES™

$\mathcal{I}$n our soup kitchens we
provide for people who are drifters.
They come for a meal, and some of them
don't eat at all. They just want to be
there in an atmosphere of peace and
tranquility. Most people don't just
want soup, they want contact where
they are appreciated, loved, feel wanted,
and find some peace in their hearts.
It's the personal touch that matters.

–SISTER DOLORES

$\mathcal{I}$f only all the hands that
reach could touch.

–MARY A. LOBERG

$\mathcal{I}$t takes courage for a
person to listen to his own
goodness and act on it.

–PABLO CASALS

$\mathcal{Y}$ou are not alone. We are all
connected. You could no more separate
yourself from humanity than a wave
could separate itself from the ocean
and still be a wave.

–GERALD JAMPOLSKY

$\mathcal{W}$e all stumble, every one of us.
That's why it's a comfort to go hand in hand.

–EMILY KIMBROUGH

LITTLE MIRACLES™

$\mathcal{W}$e cannot live only
for ourselves. A thousand fibers
connect us with our fellow man;
and along these fibers, as sympathetic
threads, our actions run as causes,
and they come back as effects.

–HERMAN MELVILLE

☆

$\mathcal{I}$f I just do my thing
and you do yours, we stand
in danger of losing each other
and ourselves. I must begin with myself,
true; but I must not end with myself.
The truth begins with two.

–WALTER TUBBS

LITTLE MIRACLES™

We need
heart-to-heart
resuscitation.
–RAM DASS

*E*mpathy is two hearts
pulling at one load.
–DAN ZADRA

*G*o ahead and cry,
I'll catch your tears.
–JILEEN RUSSELL

LITTLE MIRACLES™

$\mathscr{W}$e can do no great things;
only small things with great love.

–Mother Teresa

$\mathscr{I}$t is not our toughness
that keeps us warm at night,
but our tenderness which makes
others want to keep us warm.

–Harold Lyon

$\mathscr{D}$on't forget to love yourself.

–Soren Kierkegaard

LITTLE MIRACLES™

110

WE ARE EACH OF
US ANGELS WITH ONLY
ONE WING. AND WE CAN
ONLY FLY EMBRACING
EACH OTHER.
—Luciano De Creschenzo

INVITE ☆ EXPECT ☆ RECEIVE ☆ ENJOY

$\mathcal{G}$od doesn't comfort us to make us comfortable but to make us comforters.

–J.H. LOVETT

$\mathcal{A}$s soon as healing takes place, go out and heal somebody else.

–MAYA ANGELOU

$\mathcal{T}$hose who need your love the most are often those who appear to deserve it least.

–KEYNOTE

$\mathcal{T}$o forgive is to
find again a lost possession.

–FRIEDRICH SCHILLER

$\mathcal{T}$here is a chord in every heart
that has a sigh in it if touched right.

–OUIDA

$\mathcal{F}$orgiveness is the answer to the
child's dream of a miracle, whereby what
is broken is made whole again.

–DAG HAMMARSKJOLD

LITTLE MIRACLES™

$\mathcal{W}$hat value has
compassion if it does not take
its object in its arms.

–ANTOINE DE SAINT-EXUPERY

$\mathcal{T}$here is no such thing as
wasted affection.

–DAN ZADRA

$\mathcal{B}$e not forgetful to comfort
strangers, for thereby some have
entertained angels unawares.

–HEBREWS 13:2

LITTLE MIRACLES™

$\mathcal{I}$t is when we forget ourselves
that we do things that are most
likely to be remembered.

–UNKNOWN

$\mathcal{R}$espect is what we owe.
Love is what we give.

–PHILIP JAMES BAILEY

$\mathcal{T}$hose whom we
support hold us up in life.

–MARIE EBNER VON ESHENBACH

$\mathscr{I}$t is an uncomfortable
doctrine which the true ethics
whisper in my ear. You are happy,
they say; therefore you are called
upon to give much.

–ALBERT SCHWEITZER

☆

$\mathscr{T}$hose who give when they
are asked have waited too long.

–KOBI YAMADA

☆

$\mathscr{I}$t is one of the most beautiful
compensations of this life that the more
you give away to others, the more
you get to keep for yourself.

–UNKNOWN

LITTLE MIRACLES™

*W*hat I kept, I lost.
What I spent, I had.
What I gave, I have.
—HENRY BUCHER

*G*od's arithmetic:
Happiness adds and multiplies as
you divide it with others.
—KEYNOTE

*I*f we have no peace,
it is because we have forgotten
that we belong to each other.
—MOTHER TERESA

LITTLE MIRACLES™

$\mathcal{G}$iving never moves
in a straight line—it always
travels in circles.

–ROBERT SCHULLER

$\mathcal{H}$ave you had a
kindness shown? Pass it on.

–HENRY BURTON

$\mathcal{L}$et no one ever come to you
without leaving better.

–MOTHER TERESA

NEVER PLACE A
PERIOD WHERE GOD
HAS PLACED A
COMMA.

–Gracie Allen

INVITE ☆ EXPECT ☆ RECEIVE ☆ ENJOY

Young. Old. Just words.

–GEORGE BURNS

There are trees that
seem to die at the end of autumn.
There are also the evergreens.

–GILBERT MAXWELL

What grows never grows old.

–NOAH BENSHEA

LITTLE MIRACLES™

$\mathscr{W}$e are always the
same age inside.

–Unknown

$\mathscr{T}$hose who love deeply
never grow old; they may die of
old age, but they die young.

–Sir Arthur Wing Pinero

$\mathscr{P}$arts of you are
still in unfinished business.

–The Color Of Light

*F*ire is seen in the eyes of
the young, but it is light we see
in the old person's eyes.

–Victor Hugo

I am delighted that even at my
great age ideas come to me, the pursuit of
which would require another lifetime.

–Johann Von Goethe

*T*o be alive, to be able to see, to walk, to
have a home, music, paintings, friends—it's
all a miracle. I have adopted the technique
of living life from miracle to miracle.

–Artur Rubinstein

$\mathcal{C}$ome out of the
circle of time, and into
the circle of love.

–JALALUDIN RUMI

$\mathcal{T}$o live in the hearts we
leave behind is not to die.

–THOMAS CAMPBELL

$\mathcal{Y}$our heart has brought
great joy to many. Those hearts
can never forget you.

–FLAVIA

LITTLE MIRACLES™

It matters not how long
we live, but how.

–PHILLIP JAMES BAILEY

A span of life is nothing.
But the man or woman who lives that
span, they are something. They can fill
that tiny span with meaning, so its
quality is immeasurable, though its
quantity may be insignificant.

–CHAIM POTOK

The aim, if reached or not,
makes great the life.

–ROBERT BROWNING

LITTLE MIRACLES™

*H*ere is the test to determine if
your mission in this world is finished:
If you're alive, it isn't.

–RICHARD BACH

*N*o matter what your age or
your condition, your dreams are
renewable. Whether you're five or 105,
you have a lifetime ahead of you!

–KEYNOTE

*S*parrow, your message is clear:
it is not too late for my singing.

–TESS GALLAGHER

LITTLE MIRACLES™

The best is yet to be.

—ROBERT BROWNING

*H*ow simple
it is to see that
all the worry
in the world
cannot control
the future.
How simple
it is to see that
we can only
be happy now,
and that there
will never be a
time when it is
not now.

−GERALD JAMPOLSKY

Also available from Compendium Publishing are these spirited
and compelling companion books of great quotations.

BECAUSE OF YOU™
Celebrating the Difference You Make™
Thoughts to Inspire the People Who Inspire Us™

BRILLIANCE™
Uncommon Voices From Uncommon Women™
Thoughts to Inspire and Celebrate Your Achievements™

FOREVER REMEMBERED™
A Gift for the Grieving Heart.™
*Cherished messages of hope, love and comfort from
courageous people who have lost a loved one.*™

I BELIEVE IN YOU™
To your heart, your dream, and the difference you make.™

TO YOUR SUCCESS™
Dream • Team • Care • Dare™
Thoughts to Give Wings to Your Work and Your Dreams™

YOU'VE GOT A FRIEND™
Thoughts to Celebrate the Joy of Friendship™

WHATEVER IT TAKES™
A Journey into the Heart of Human Achievement™
Thoughts to Inspire and Celebrate Your Commitment to Excellence™

These books may be ordered directly from the publisher (800) 914-3327.
But please try your bookstore first!

www.compendiuminc.com